T0045648

ESSENTIAL ELEMENTS
FOR BAND

COMPREHENSIVE BAND METHOD

TIM LAUTZENHEISER
PAUL LAVENDER

JOHN HIGGINS
TOM C. RHODES

CHARLES MENGHINI
DON BIERSCHENK

Band is… **M**aking music with a family of lifelong friends.
Understanding how commitment and dedication lead to success.
Sharing the joy and rewards of working together.
Individuals who develop self-confidence.
Creativity—expressing yourself in a universal language.
Band is…**MUSIC!**
Strike up the band,
Tim Lautzenheiser

HISTORY OF THE ALTO SAXOPHONE

In the 1840s, Adolphe Sax invented the saxophone family. In today's concert band, saxophones play harmonies and blend with other band instruments. Saxophones are also very popular jazz and solo instruments.

The saxophone family includes the Bb Soprano, Eb Alto (the most common), Bb Tenor, Eb Baritone and Bb Bass Saxophone. Fingerings are virtually the same on all saxophones, making it possible to play any saxophone.

John Philip Sousa wrote for saxophones in his band compositions. Bizet, Ravel, Debussy and Prokofiev included saxophones in their orchestral writing. Duke Ellington's jazz arrangements greatly defined the unique sound of the instruments, both in solo and ensemble playing.

Some famous saxophone performers are Eugene Rousseau, Sigurd Rascher and David Sanborn.

ISBN 978-0-634-00317-2

HAL•LEONARD®
CORPORATION

7777 W. BLUEMOUND RD. P.O. BOX 13819 MILWAUKEE, WI 53213

THE BASICS

Posture

Sit on the edge of your chair, and always keep your:
- Spine straight and tall
- Shoulders back and relaxed
- Feet flat on the floor

Breathing & Airstream

Breathing is a natural thing we all do constantly. To discover the correct airstream to play your instrument:
- Place the palm of your hand near your mouth.
- Inhale deeply through the corners of your mouth, keeping your shoulders steady. Your waist should expand like a balloon.
- Slowly whisper "too" as you gradually exhale air into your palm.

The air you feel is the airstream. It produces sound through the instrument. Your tongue is like a faucet or valve that releases the airstream.

Producing The Essential Tone

Your embouchure *(ahm´-bah-shure)* is your mouth's position on the mouthpiece of the instrument. A good embouchure takes time and effort, so carefully follow these steps for success:

REED PLACEMENT
- Put the thin end of the reed in your mouth to moisten it thoroughly.
- Looking at the flat side of the mouthpiece, the ligature screws extend to your right. Slide the ligature up with your thumb.
- Place the flat side of the reed against the mouthpiece under the ligature.
- Lower the ligature and position the reed so that only a hairline of the mouthpiece can be seen above the reed.
- Gently tighten the ligature screws.

EMBOUCHURE
- Moisten your lips and roll the lower lip over your bottom teeth.
- Center the mouthpiece on your lips and place it in your mouth about 1/2 inch.
- Place your upper teeth directly on the mouthpiece. The reed rests on the lower lip over the teeth.
- Close your mouth around the mouthpiece, like a rubber band. Your facial muscles all support and cushion your lips on the mouthpiece.
- Keep your chin down and slightly relaxed.

Taking Care Of Your Instrument

Before putting your instrument back in its case after playing, do the following:
- Remove the reed, wipe off excess moisture and return it to the reed case.
- Remove the mouthpiece and wipe the inside with a clean cloth. Once a week, wash the mouthpiece with warm tap water. Dry thoroughly.
- Loosen the neck screw and remove the neck. Shake out excess moisture and dry the neck with a neck cleaner.
- Drop the weight of a chamois or cotton swab into the bell. Pull the swab through the body several times. Return the instrument to its case.
- Your case is designed to hold only specific objects. If you try to force anything else into the case, it may damage your instrument.

MOUTHPIECE WORKOUT

Form your embouchure around the mouthpiece, and take a deep breath without raising your shoulders. Whisper "too" and gradually exhale your full airstream. Strive for an even tone.

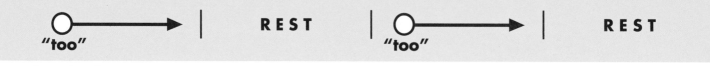

Getting It Together

If you just played the MOUTHPIECE WORKOUT, begin by carefully removing the reed. Otherwise, take the reed from its case.

Step 1 Carefully put the thin end of the reed in your mouth to moisten thoroughly. Rub a small amount of cork grease on the neck cork, if needed. Clean hands.

Step 2 Hold the body of the saxophone near its upper end and remove the end plug. Loosen the neck screw and gently twist the neck into the body. Be careful not to bend any keys. Tighten the neck screw.

Step 3 Carefully twist the mouthpiece on the neck so that approximately 1/2 of the cork remains uncovered. Place the reed on the mouthpiece (see page 2).

Step 4 Place the neck strap around your neck and attach the hook to the ring on the back of the saxophone. Adjust the length of the strap so you can comfortably put the mouthpiece in your mouth.

mouthpiece

ligature

cork

neck

neck screw

octave key

left thumb rest

body

bell

right thumb rest

Step 5 Place your right thumb under the thumb rest. Put your left thumb diagonally across the left thumb rest. Your fingers should curve naturally. Hold the instrument as shown at left:

READING MUSIC   Identify and draw each of these symbols:

Music Staff

The **music staff** has 5 lines and 4 spaces where notes and rests are written.

Ledger Lines

Ledger lines extend the music staff. Notes on ledger lines can be above or below the staff.

Measures & Bar Lines

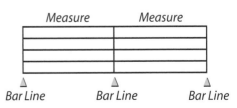

Measure   *Measure*

Bar Line   *Bar Line*   *Bar Line*

Bar lines divide the music staff into **measures**.

Long Tone ⟶ To begin, we'll use a special "Long Tone" note. Hold the tone until your teacher tells you to rest. Practice long tones each day to develop your sound.

1. THE FIRST NOTE

Hold each long tone until your teacher tells you to rest.

△ *To play "D," place your fingers on the keys as shown.*

The Beat

The **beat** is the pulse of music, and like your heartbeat it should remain very steady. Counting aloud and foot-tapping help us maintain a steady beat. Tap your foot **down** on each number and **up** on each "&."

One beat = 1   &
            ↓   ↑

Notes And Rests

Notes tell us how high or low to play by their placement on a line or space of the music staff, and how long to play by their shape. **Rests** tell us to count silent beats.

♩ **Quarter Note   =   1 beat**

𝄽 **Quarter Rest   =   1 silent beat**

2. COUNT AND PLAY

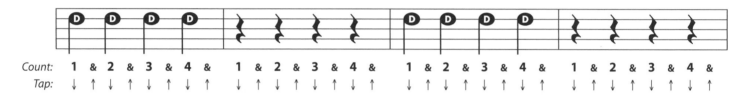

| Count: | 1 | & | 2 | & | 3 | & | 4 | & | 1 | & | 2 | & | 3 | & | 4 | & | 1 | & | 2 | & | 3 | & | 4 | & | 1 | & | 2 | & | 3 | & | 4 | & |
| Tap: | ↓ | ↑ | ↓ | ↑ | ↓ | ↑ | ↓ | ↑ | ↓ | ↑ | ↓ | ↑ | ↓ | ↑ | ↓ | ↑ | ↓ | ↑ | ↓ | ↑ | ↓ | ↑ | ↓ | ↑ | ↓ | ↑ | ↓ | ↑ | ↓ | ↑ | ↓ | ↑ |

3. A NEW NOTE

Look for the fingering diagram with each new note.

4. TWO'S A TEAM

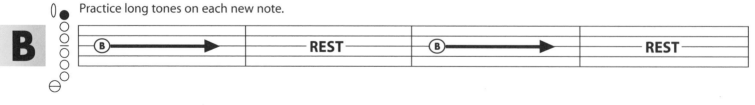

Count & Tap: 1 & 2 & 3 & 4 &   1 & 2 & 3 & 4 &   1 & 2 & 3 & 4 &   1 & 2 & 3 & 4 &

5. HEADING DOWN

Practice long tones on each new note.

6. MOVING ON UP

Count & Tap: 1 & 2 & 3 & 4 &   1 & 2 & 3 & 4 &   1 & 2 & 3 & 4 &   1 & 2 & 3 & 4 &

| **Double Bar** | indicates the end of a piece of music. | **Repeat Sign** | Without stopping, play once again from the beginning. |

7. THE LONG HAUL

Double Bar ▾

A | A ————→ | REST | A ————→ | REST |

8. FOUR BY FOUR

Repeat Sign ▾

A A A A | B | D D D D | C

Count & Tap: 1 & 2 & 3 & 4 & 1 & 2 & 3 & 4 & 1 & 2 & 3 & 4 & 1 & 2 & 3 & 4 &

9. TOUCHDOWN

G | G ————→ | REST | G ————→ | REST |

10. THE FAB FIVE

G G G G | A | D D C C | B

1 & 2 & 3 & 4 & 1 & 2 & 3 & 4 & 1 & 2 & 3 & 4 & 1 & 2 & 3 & 4 &

Treble Clef

(G Clef) indicates the position of note names on a music staff: Second line is G.

Time Signature

indicates how many beats per measure and what kind of note gets one beat.

= **4 beats** per measure
= **Quarter** note gets one beat

Note Names

Each note is on a line or space of the staff. These note names are indicated by the Treble Clef.

THEORY

Sharp	♯	raises the note and remains in effect for the entire measure.
Flat	♭	lowers the note and remains in effect for the entire measure.
Natural	♮	cancels a flat (♭) or sharp (♯) and remains in effect for the entire measure.

11. READING THE NOTES   *Compare this to exercise 10, THE FAB FIVE.*

1 & 2 & 3 & 4 & 1 & 2 & 3 & 4 & 1 & 2 & 3 & 4 & 1 & 2 & 3 & 4 &

12. FIRST FLIGHT

13. ESSENTIAL ELEMENTS QUIZ   *Fill in the remaining note names before playing.*

G A B __ __ __ __ __ __ __

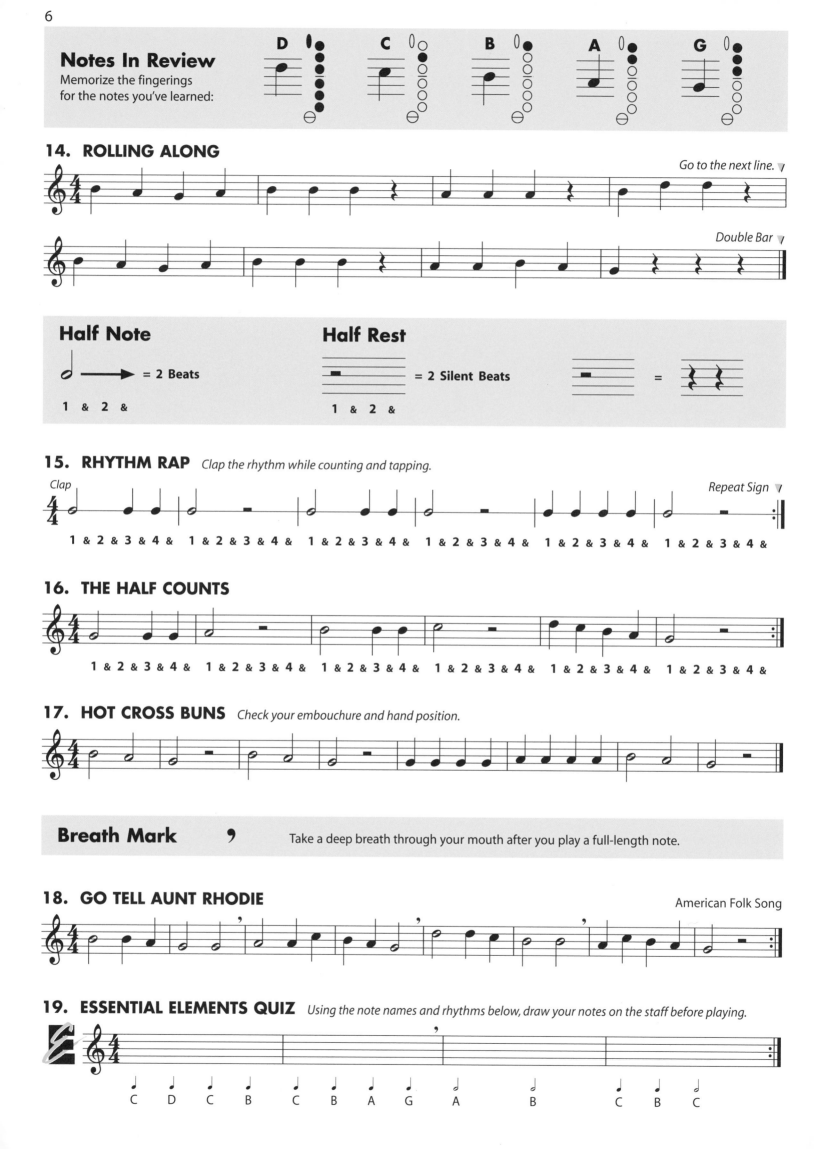

Fermata　　　⌢　　　Hold the note (or rest) longer than normal.

27. REACHING HIGHER – New Note

Practice long tones on each new note.　　　　　　　　　　　　　　*Fermata*

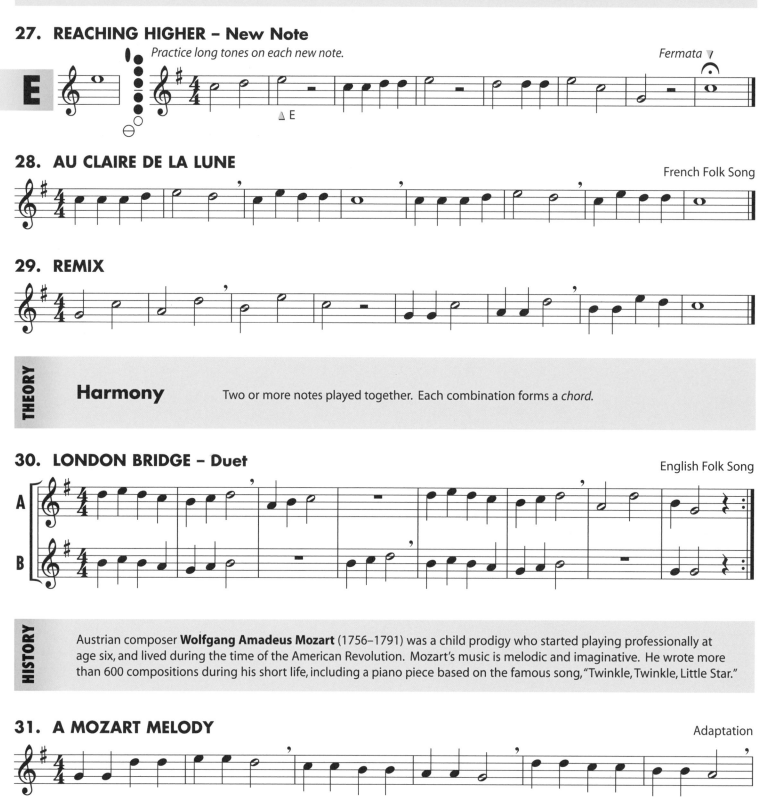

28. AU CLAIRE DE LA LUNE

French Folk Song

29. REMIX

THEORY

Harmony

Two or more notes played together. Each combination forms a *chord*.

30. LONDON BRIDGE – Duet

English Folk Song

HISTORY

Austrian composer **Wolfgang Amadeus Mozart** (1756–1791) was a child prodigy who started playing professionally at age six, and lived during the time of the American Revolution. Mozart's music is melodic and imaginative. He wrote more than 600 compositions during his short life, including a piano piece based on the famous song, "Twinkle, Twinkle, Little Star."

31. A MOZART MELODY

Adaptation

32. ESSENTIAL ELEMENTS QUIZ

Draw these symbols where they belong and write in the note names before you play:

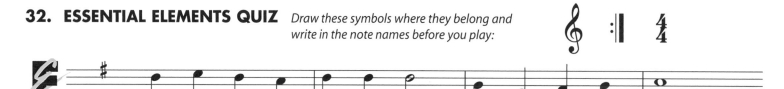

33. DEEP POCKETS – New Note

34. DOODLE ALL DAY

35. JUMP ROPE

Pick-Up Notes

One or more notes that come before the first *full* measure. The beats of Pick-Up Notes are subtracted from the last measure.

36. A-TISKET, A-TASKET

Pick-up note

4 &   1 & 2 & 3 & 4 &   1 & 2 & 3 &

Dynamics

f – *forte* (play loudly)   *mf* – *mezzo forte* (play moderately loud)   *p* – *piano* (play softly)

Remember to use full breath support to control your tone at all dynamic levels.

37. LOUD AND SOFT

Clap

38. JINGLE BELLS *Keep your fingers close to the keys, curved naturally.*   J. S. Pierpont

39. MY DREYDL *Use full breath support at all dynamic levels.*   Traditional Hanukkah Song

Eighth Notes

Each Eighth Note = ½ Beat
2 Eighth Notes = 1 Beat
Play on down and up taps.

1 &

1 & 2 &

Two or more Eighth Notes have a *beam* across the stems.

▼ Beam

=

40. RHYTHM RAP *Clap the rhythm while counting and tapping.*

41. EIGHTH NOTE JAM

42. SKIP TO MY LOU

American Folk Song

43. LONG, LONG AGO *Good posture improves your sound. Always sit straight and tall.*

44. OH, SUSANNA

Stephen Collins Foster

HISTORY

Italian composer **Gioacchino Rossini** (1792–1868) began composing as a teenager and was very proficient on the piano, viola and horn. He wrote "William Tell" at age 37 as the last of his forty operas, and its familiar theme is still heard today on radio and television.

45. ESSENTIAL ELEMENTS QUIZ — WILLIAM TELL

Gioacchino Rossini

Time Signature

$\frac{2}{4}$

= **2 beats** per measure
= **Quarter** note gets one beat

Conducting

Practice conducting this two-beat pattern.

46. RHYTHM RAP

Clap

1 & 2 & 1 & 2 & 1 & 2 & 1 & 2 & 1 & 2 & 1 & 2 & 1 & 2 & 1 & 2 &

47. TWO BY TWO

1 & 2 & 1 & 2 & 1 & 2 & 1 & 2 & 1 & 2 & 1 & 2 & 1 & 2 & 1 & 2 &

Tempo Markings

Tempo is the speed of music. Tempo markings are usually written above the staff, in Italian.

Allegro – Fast tempo   **Moderato** – Medium tempo   **Andante** – Slower walking tempo

48. HIGH SCHOOL CADETS – March

John Philip Sousa

Allegro

f

Reproduced by Permission of Boosey & Hawkes Music Publishers Ltd.

49. HEY, HO! NOBODY'S HOME – New Note

E

Moderato

mf   △ E

Dynamics

Crescendo (gradually louder)   *Decrescendo* or *Diminuendo* (gradually softer)

50. CLAP THE DYNAMICS

Clap

p ———— *f*   *f* ———— *p*

51. PLAY THE DYNAMICS

p ———— *f*   *f* ———— *p*

PERFORMANCE SPOTLIGHT

52. PERFORMANCE WARM-UPS

TONE BUILDER

RHYTHM ETUDE

RHYTHM RAP

Clap

Stomp!

CHORALE

Andante

53. AURA LEE – Duet or Band Arrangement

(Part A = Melody, Part B = Harmony)

George R. Poulton

Andante

54. FRÈRE JACQUES – Round *(When group A reaches ②, groups B begins at ①)*

Moderato

French Folk Song

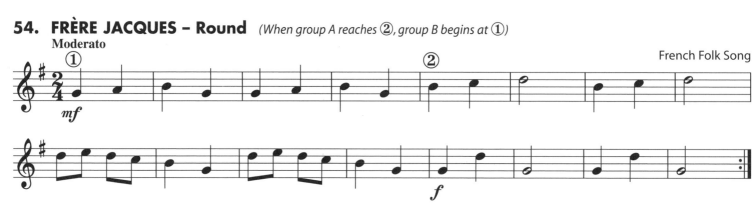

PERFORMANCE SPOTLIGHT

55. WHEN THE SAINTS GO MARCHING IN – Band Arrangement

Arr. by John Higgins

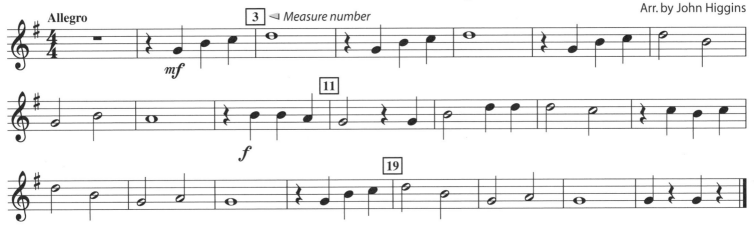

56. OLD MACDONALD HAD A BAND – Section Feature

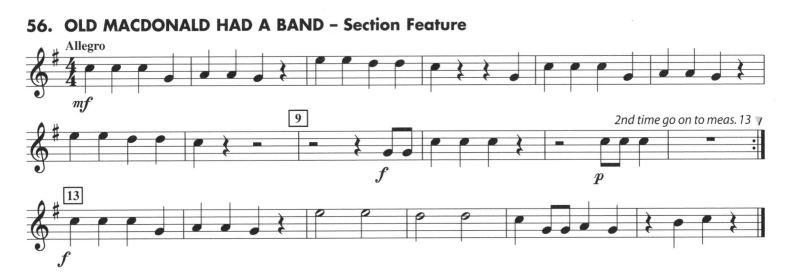

57. ODE TO JOY (from Symphony No. 9)

Ludwig van Beethoven
Arr. by John Higgins

58. HARD ROCK BLUES – Encore

John Higgins

14

| **Tie** | A curved line connecting notes of the same pitch. Play one note for the combined counts of the tied notes. |  = 2 Beats |

59. FIT TO BE TIED

2 beats △

60. ALOUETTE

French-Canadian Folk Song

3 beats △

Dotted Half Note

♩. ⟶ = 3 Beats
1 & 2 & 3 &

♩. ◄ Dot
A dot adds half the value of the note.

♩ ⌣ ♩ = ♩.
2 beats + 1 beat = 3 beats

61. ALOUETTE – THE SEQUEL

French-Canadian Folk Song

62. CAMPTOWN RACES

Stephen Collins Foster

Allegro

mf

63. NEW DIRECTIONS – New Note

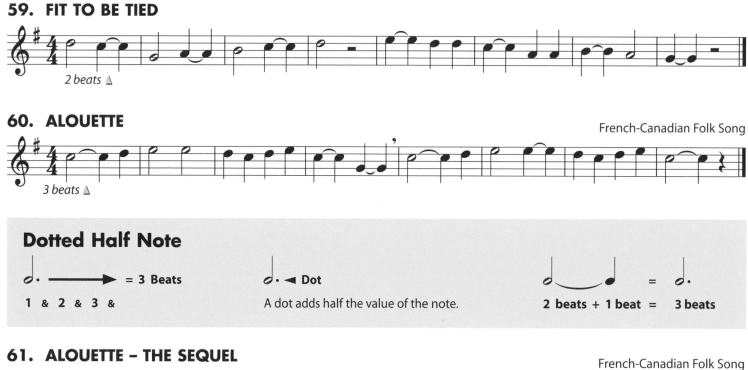

D

△ D

64. THE NOBLES *Always use a full airstream. Keep fingers above the keys, curved naturally.*

3 beats △

65. ESSENTIAL ELEMENTS QUIZ

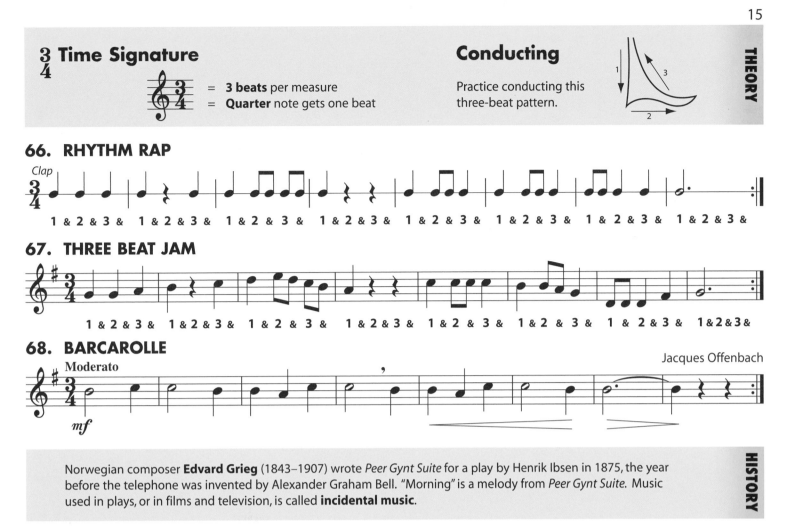

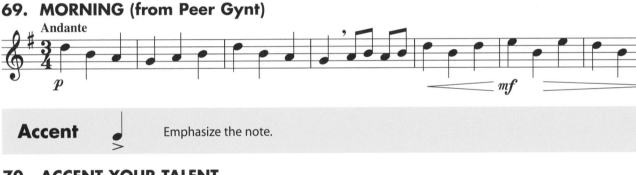

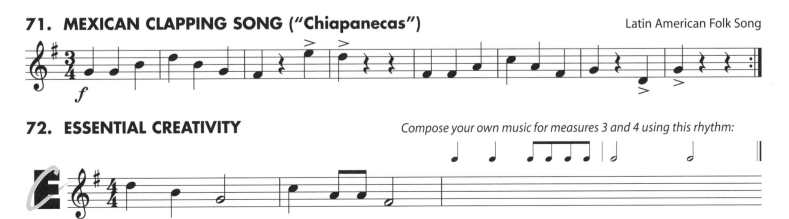

THEORY

Accidental

Any sharp, flat or natural sign which appears in the music without being in the key signature is called an **accidental**.

Natural ♮

A **natural** sign cancels a flat (♭) or sharp (♯) and remains in effect for the entire measure.

73. HOT MUFFINS – New Note

F

Natural applies to all F's in measure.

△ F♯

74. COSSACK DANCE

Allegro

75. BASIC BLUES – New Note

F

Natural applies to all F's in measure.

THEORY

New Key Signature

This Key Signature indicates the *Key of C* (no sharps or flats).

1st & 2nd Endings

| 1. | 2. |

Play through the 1st Ending. Then play the repeated section of music, **skipping** the 1st Ending and playing the 2nd Ending.

76. HIGH FLYING

Moderato

1.

2nd time

2.

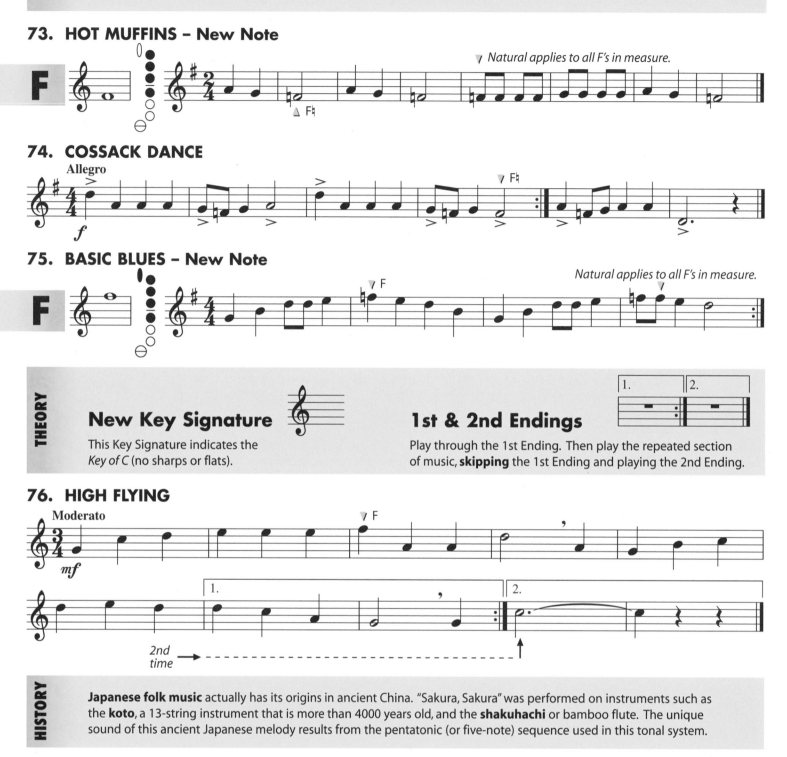

HISTORY

Japanese folk music actually has its origins in ancient China. "Sakura, Sakura" was performed on instruments such as the **koto**, a 13-string instrument that is more than 4000 years old, and the **shakuhachi** or bamboo flute. The unique sound of this ancient Japanese melody results from the pentatonic (or five-note) sequence used in this tonal system.

77. SAKURA, SAKURA – Band Arrangement

Japanese Folk Song
Arr. by John Higgins

Andante

17

78. UP ON A HOUSETOP

Check Key Signature

79. JOLLY OLD ST. NICK – Duet

See page 9 for additional holiday music, MY DREYDL and JINGLE BELLS.

80. THE BIG AIRSTREAM – New Note

81. WALTZ THEME (THE MERRY WIDOW WALTZ)

Franz Lehar

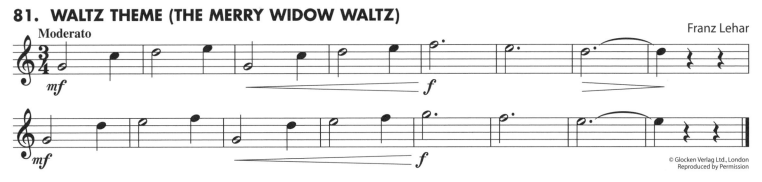

© Glocken Verlag Ltd., London
Reproduced by Permission

82. AIR TIME

83. DOWN BY THE STATION

84. ESSENTIAL ELEMENTS QUIZ

85. ESSENTIAL CREATIVITY *Using these notes, improvise your own rhythms:*

18

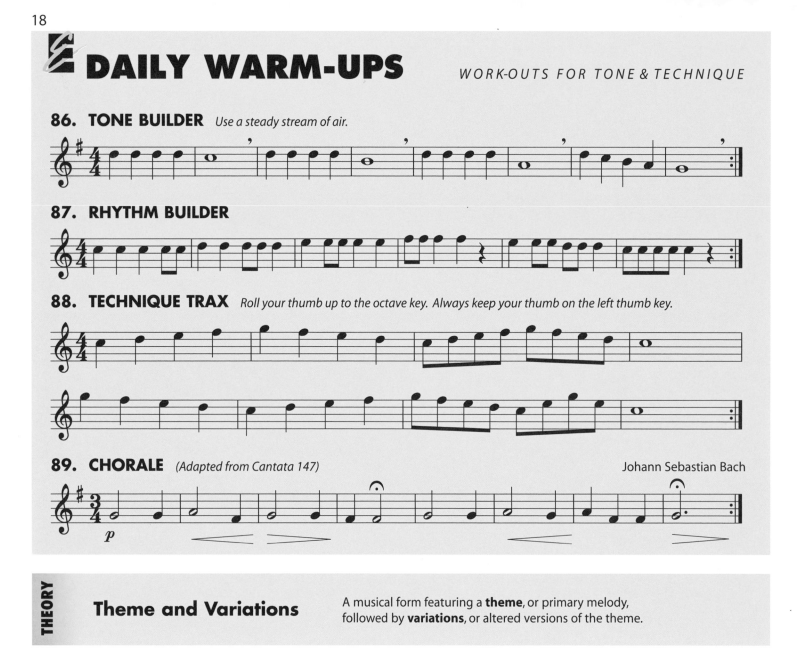

DAILY WARM-UPS — WORK-OUTS FOR TONE & TECHNIQUE

86. TONE BUILDER *Use a steady stream of air.*

87. RHYTHM BUILDER

88. TECHNIQUE TRAX *Roll your thumb up to the octave key. Always keep your thumb on the left thumb key.*

89. CHORALE *(Adapted from Cantata 147)* Johann Sebastian Bach

THEORY

Theme and Variations

A musical form featuring a **theme**, or primary melody, followed by **variations**, or altered versions of the theme.

90. VARIATIONS ON A FAMILIAR THEME

D.C. al Fine

At the **D.C. al Fine** play again from the beginning, stopping at **Fine** (fee'- nay).
D.C. is the abbreviation for **Da Capo**, or "to the beginning," and **Fine** means "the end."

91. BANANA BOAT SONG

Caribbean Folk Song

Sharp

A **sharp** sign raises the pitch of a note by a half-step. The note C-sharp sounds a half-step above C, and all C's become C-sharps for the rest of the measure where they occur.

92. RAZOR'S EDGE – New Note

93. THE MUSIC BOX

African-American spirituals originated in the 1700's, midway through the period of slavery in the United States. One of the largest categories of true American folk music, these primarily religious songs were sung and passed on for generations without being written down. The first collection of spirituals was published in 1867, four years after The Emancipation Proclamation was signed into law.

HISTORY

94. EZEKIEL SAW THE WHEEL

African-American Spiritual

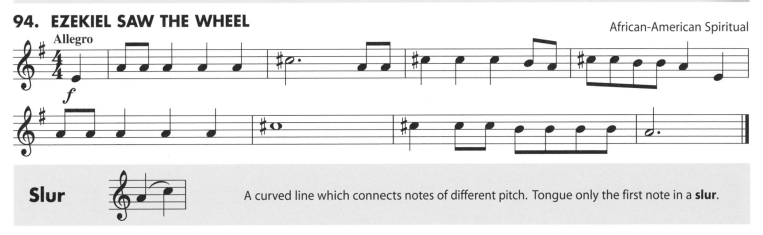

Slur

A curved line which connects notes of different pitch. Tongue only the first note in a **slur**.

95. SMOOTH OPERATOR

△ Slur 2 notes – tongue only the first.

96. GLIDING ALONG

△ Slur 4 notes – tongue only the first.

Ragtime is an American music style that was popular from the 1890's until the time of World War I. This early form of jazz brought fame to pianists like "Jelly Roll" Morton and Scott Joplin, who wrote "The Entertainer" and "Maple Leaf Rag." Surprisingly, the style was incorporated into some orchestral music by Igor Stravinsky and Claude Debussy. The trombones now learn to play a *glissando*, a technique used in ragtime and other styles of music.

HISTORY

97. TROMBONE RAG

98. ESSENTIAL ELEMENTS QUIZ

99. TAKE THE LEAD – New Note

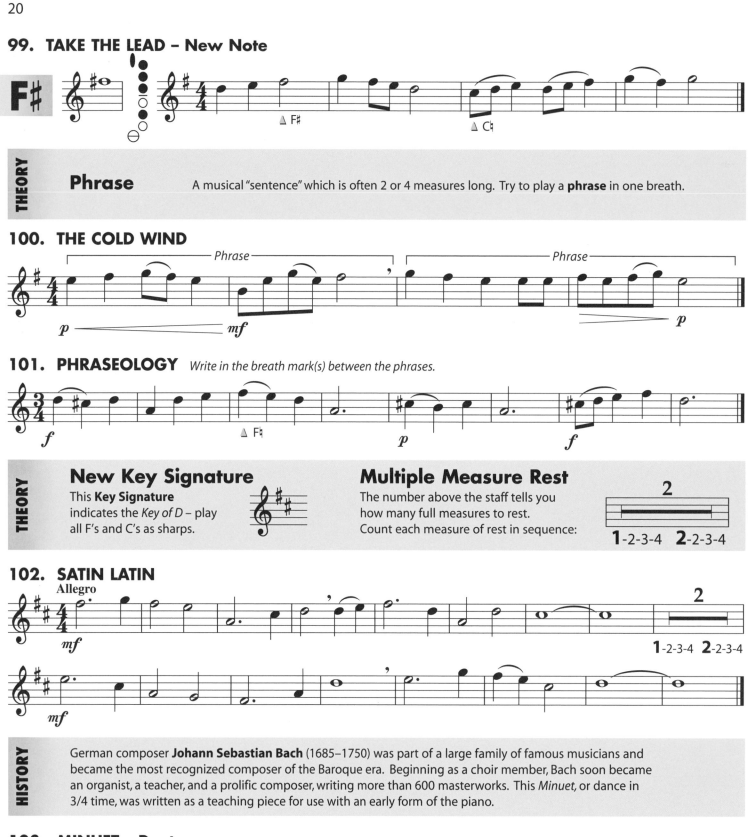

Phrase

A musical "sentence" which is often 2 or 4 measures long. Try to play a **phrase** in one breath.

---

100. THE COLD WIND

101. PHRASEOLOGY
Write in the breath mark(s) between the phrases.

New Key Signature

This **Key Signature** indicates the *Key of D* – play all F's and C's as sharps.

Multiple Measure Rest

The number above the staff tells you how many full measures to rest.
Count each measure of rest in sequence:

1-2-3-4 **2**-2-3-4

---

102. SATIN LATIN

Allegro

1-2-3-4 **2**-2-3-4

German composer **Johann Sebastian Bach** (1685–1750) was part of a large family of famous musicians and became the most recognized composer of the Baroque era. Beginning as a choir member, Bach soon became an organist, a teacher, and a prolific composer, writing more than 600 masterworks. This *Minuet,* or dance in 3/4 time, was written as a teaching piece for use with an early form of the piano.

---

103. MINUET – Duet

Johann Sebastian Bach

Moderato

A

B

---

104. ESSENTIAL CREATIVITY
This melody can be played in 3/4 or 4/4. Pencil in either time signature, draw the bar lines and play. Now erase the bar lines and try the other time signature. Do the phrases sound different?

105. NATURALLY

Austrian composer **Franz Peter Schubert** (1797–1828) lived a shorter life than any other great composer, but he created an incredible amount of music: more than 600 art-songs (concert music for voice and accompaniment), ten symphonies, chamber music, operas, choral works and piano pieces. His "March Militaire" was originally a piano duet.

HISTORY

106. MARCH MILITAIRE

Franz Schubert

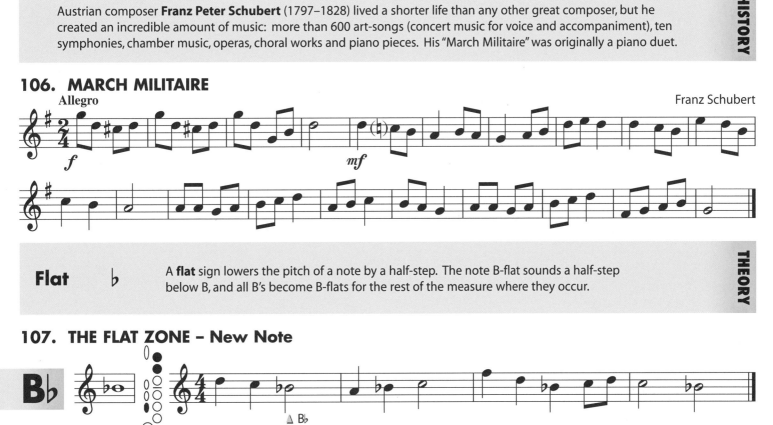

Flat ♭ — A **flat** sign lowers the pitch of a note by a half-step. The note B-flat sounds a half-step below B, and all B's become B-flats for the rest of the measure where they occur.

THEORY

107. THE FLAT ZONE – New Note

108. ON TOP OF OLD SMOKEY

American Folk Song

Boogie-woogie is a style of the **blues**, and it was first recorded by pianist Clarence "Pine Top" Smith in 1928, one year after Charles Lindbergh's solo flight across the Atlantic. A form of jazz, blues music features altered notes and is usually written in 12-measure verses, like "Bottom Bass Boogie."

HISTORY

109. BOTTOM BASS BOOGIE – Duet

PERFORMANCE SPOTLIGHT

Solo with Piano Accompaniment

You can perform this solo with or without a piano accompanist. Play it for the band, the school or your family. It is part of **Symphony No. 9 ("From The New World")** by Czech composer **Antonin Dvořák** (1841–1904). He wrote it while visiting America in 1893, and was inspired to include melodies from American folksongs and spirituals. This is the **Largo** (or "very slow tempo") theme.

118. THEME FROM "NEW WORLD SYMPHONY"

Antonin Dvořák

Great musicians give encouragement to fellow performers. On this page, clarinetists learn their instruments' upper register in the "Grenadilla Gorilla Jumps" (named after the grenadilla wood used to make clarinets). Brass players learn lip slurs, a new warm-up pattern. The success of your band depends on everyone's effort and encouragement.

119. GRENADILLA GORILLA JUMP No. 1

120. JUMPIN' UP AND DOWN

121. GRENADILLA GORILLA JUMP No. 2 – New Note

A

122. JUMPIN' FOR JOY

123. GRENADILLA GORILLA JUMP No. 3

124. JUMPIN' JACKS

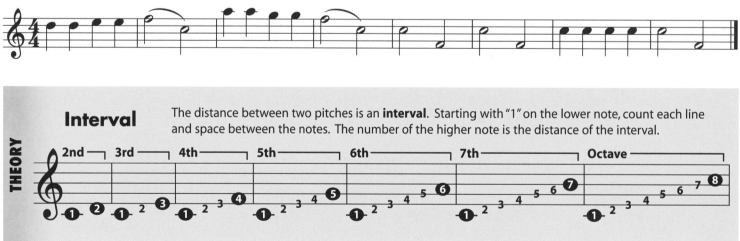

THEORY

Interval

The distance between two pitches is an **interval**. Starting with "1" on the lower note, count each line and space between the notes. The number of the higher note is the distance of the interval.

2nd   3rd   4th   5th   6th   7th   Octave

125. ESSENTIAL ELEMENTS QUIZ
Write in the numbers of the intervals, counting up from the lower notes.

Intervals: 2nd

126. GRENADILLA GORILLA JUMP No. 4

127. THREE IS THE COUNT

128. GRENADILLA GORILLA JUMP No. 5

129. TECHNIQUE TRAX

130. CROSSING OVER

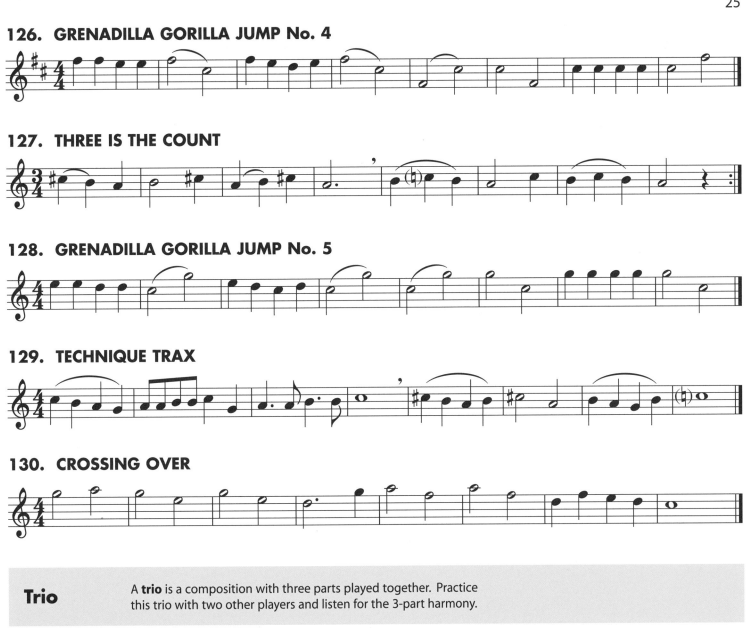

Trio   A **trio** is a composition with three parts played together. Practice this trio with two other players and listen for the 3-part harmony.

131. KUM BAH YAH – Trio   *Always check the key signature.*

African Folk Song

Repeat Signs

Repeat the section of music enclosed by the **repeat signs**.
(If 1st and 2nd endings are used, they are played as usual — but go back only to the first repeat sign, not to the beginning.)

132. MICHAEL ROW THE BOAT ASHORE

African-American Spiritual

133. AUSTRIAN WALTZ

Austrian Folk Song

134. BOTANY BAY

Australian Folk Song

THEORY

C Time Signature

= **Common Time**
(Same as 4/4)

Conducting

Practice conducting this four-beat pattern.

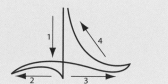

135. TECHNIQUE TRAX *Practice at all dynamic levels.*

136. FINLANDIA

Jean Sibelius

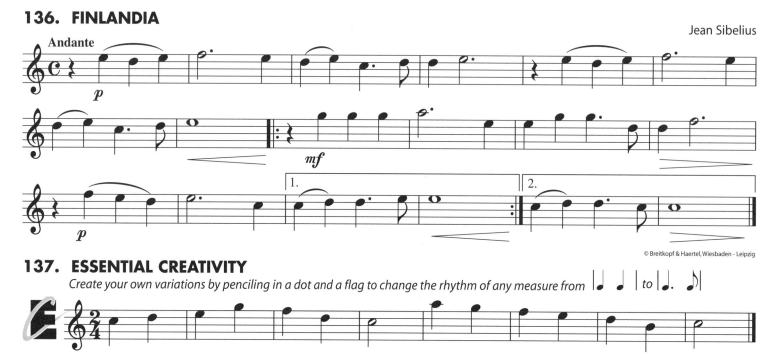

© Breitkopf & Haertel, Wiesbaden - Leipzig

137. ESSENTIAL CREATIVITY

Create your own variations by penciling in a dot and a flag to change the rhythm of any measure from ♩ ♩ *to* ♩. ♪

138. EASY GORILLA JUMPS

139. TECHNIQUE TRAX *Always check the key signature.*

140. MORE TECHNIQUE TRAX

141. GERMAN FOLK SONG

142. THE SAINTS GO MARCHIN' AGAIN

James Black and Katherine Purvis

143. LOWLAND GORILLA WALK

144. SMOOTH SAILING

145. MORE GORILLA JUMPS

146. FULL COVERAGE

THEORY

Scale

A **scale** is a sequence of notes in ascending or descending order. Like a musical "ladder," each step is the next consecutive note in the key. This scale is in your Key of G (one sharp), so the top and bottom notes are both G's. The interval between the G's is an octave.

147. CONCERT B♭ SCALE (Alto Saxophone – G SCALE)

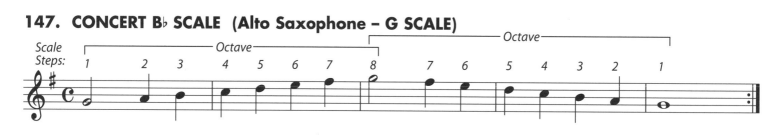

THEORY

Chord & Arpeggio

When two or more notes are played together, they form a **chord** or **harmony**. This G chord is built from the 1st, 3rd and 5th steps of the G scale. The 8th step is the same as the 1st, but it is an octave higher. An **arpeggio** is a "broken" chord whose notes are played individually.

148. IN HARMONY
Divide the notes of the chords between band members and play together. Does the arpeggio sound like a chord?

149. SCALE AND ARPEGGIO

HISTORY

Austrian composer **Franz Josef Haydn** (1732–1809) wrote 104 symphonies. Many of these works had nicknames and included brilliant, unique effects for their time. His Symphony No. 94 was named "The Surprise Symphony" because the soft second movement included a sudden loud dynamic, intended to wake up an often sleepy audience. Pay special attention to dynamics when you play this famous theme.

150. THEME FROM "SURPRISE SYMPHONY"

Franz Josef Haydn

151. ESSENTIAL ELEMENTS QUIZ – THE STREETS OF LAREDO

American Folk Song

Write in the note names before you play.

PERFORMANCE SPOTLIGHT

152. SCHOOL SPIRIT – Band Arrangement

W.T. Purdy
Arr. by John Higgins

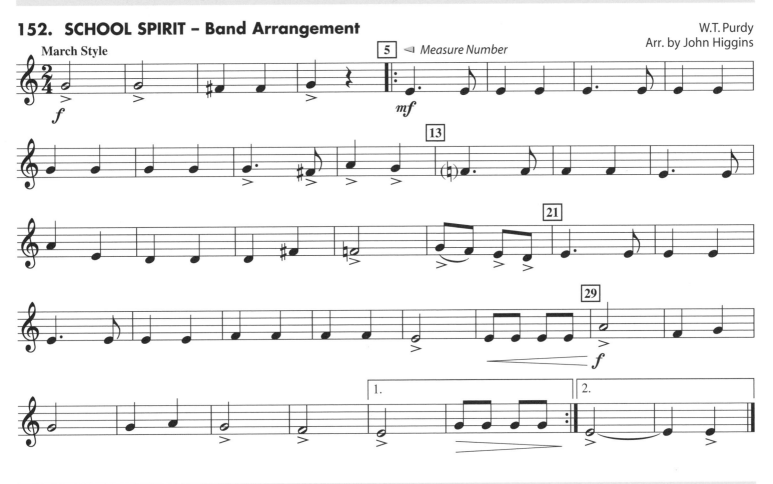

Soli

When playing music marked **Soli**, you are part of a group "solo" or group feature. Listen carefully in "Carnival of Venice," and name the instruments that play the Soli part at each indicated measure number.

153. CARNIVAL OF VENICE – Band Arrangement

Julius Benedict
Arr. by John Higgins

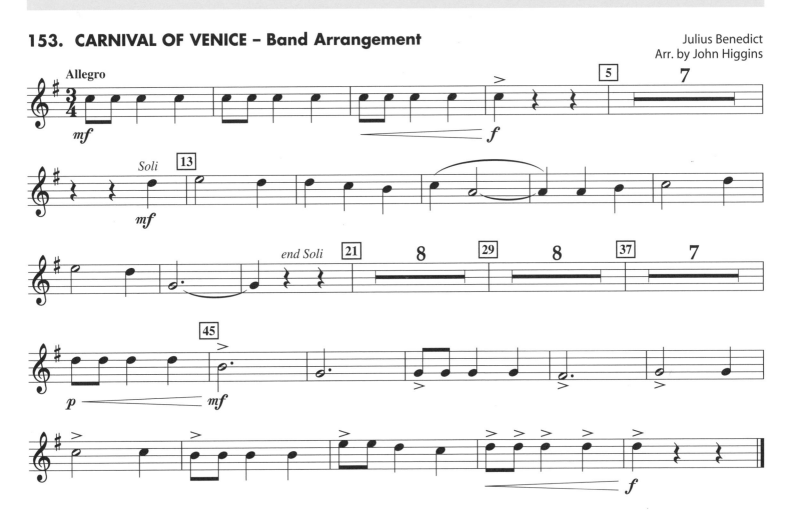

30

DAILY WARM-UPS

WORK-OUTS FOR TONE & TECHNIQUE

154. RANGE AND FLEXIBILITY BUILDER

155. TECHNIQUE TRAX

156. CHORALE

Johann Sebastian Bach

157. HATIKVAH

Israeli National Anthem

165. DANCING MELODY – New Note

HISTORY

American composer and conductor **John Philip Sousa** (1854–1932) wrote 136 marches. Known as "The March King," Sousa wrote *The Stars And Stripes Forever, Semper Fidelis, The Washington Post* and many other patriotic works. Sousa's band performed all over the country, and his fame helped boost the popularity of bands in America. Here is a melody from his famous *El Capitan* operetta and march.

166. EL CAPITAN

John Philip Sousa

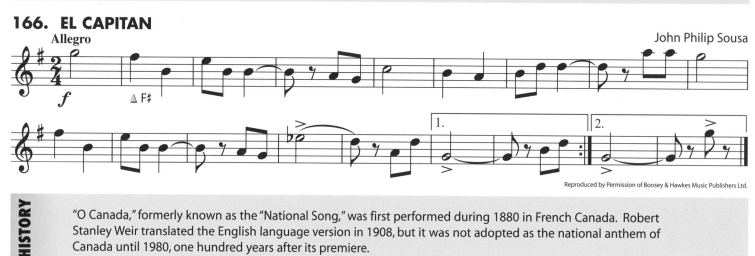

Reproduced by Permission of Boosey & Hawkes Music Publishers Ltd.

HISTORY

"O Canada," formerly known as the "National Song," was first performed during 1880 in French Canada. Robert Stanley Weir translated the English language version in 1908, but it was not adopted as the national anthem of Canada until 1980, one hundred years after its premiere.

167. O CANADA

Calixa Lavallee,
l'Hon. Judge Routhier
and Justice R.S. Weir

168. ESSENTIAL ELEMENTS QUIZ – METER MANIA *Count and clap before playing. Can you conduct this?*

Enharmonics

Two notes that are written differently, but sound the same (and played with the same fingering) are called **enharmonics**. Your fingering chart on pages 46–47 shows the fingerings for the enharmonic notes on your instrument.

On a piano keyboard, each black key is both a flat and a sharp:

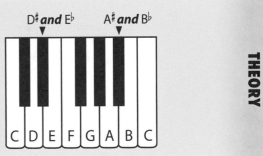

169. SNAKE CHARMER   *Enharmonic notes use the same fingering.*

E♭/D♯

170. DARK SHADOWS

△ Pick-up note

171. CLOSE ENCOUNTERS   *Enharmonic notes use the same fingering.*

B♭/A♯

172. MARCH SLAV

Peter Illyich Tchaikovsky

Largo

173. NOTES IN DISGUISE

Chromatic Notes

Chromatic notes are altered with sharps, flats and natural signs which are not in the key signature. The smallest distance between two notes is a half-step, and a scale made up of consecutive half-steps is called a **chromatic scale**.

174. HALF-STEPPIN'

F♯

Alternate fingering

F♯ Alternate fingering

HISTORY

French composer **Camille Saint-Saëns** (1835–1921) wrote music for virtually every medium: operas, suites, symphonies and chamber works. The "Egyptian Dance" is one of the main themes from his famous opera *Samson et Delilah*. The opera was written in the same year that Thomas Edison invented the phonograph—1877.

175. EGYPTIAN DANCE *Watch for enharmonics.*

Camille Saint-Saëns

176. SILVER MOON BOAT

Chinese Folk Song

HISTORY

German composer **Ludwig van Beethoven** (1770–1827) is considered to be one of the world's greatest composers, despite becoming completely deaf in 1802. Although he could not hear his music the way we can, he could "hear" it in his mind. As a testament to his greatness, his Symphony No. 9 (p. 13) was performed as the finale to the ceremony celebrating the reunification of Germany in 1990. This is the theme from his Symphony No. 7, second movement.

177. THEME FROM SYMPHONY NO. 7 – Duet

Ludwig van Beethoven

Russian composer **Peter Illyich Tchaikovsky** (1840–1893) wrote six symphonies and hundreds of other works including *The Nutcracker* ballet. He was a master at writing brilliant settings of folk music, and his original melodies are among the most popular of all time. His *1812 Overture* and *Capriccio Italien* were both written in 1880, the year after Thomas Edison developed the practical electric light bulb.

178. CAPRICCIO ITALIEN   *Always check the key signature.*

Peter Illyich Tchaikovsky

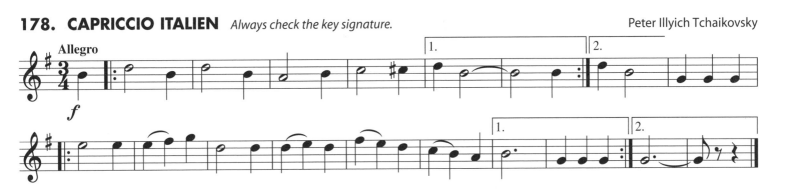

179. AMERICAN PATROL

F.W. Meacham

180. WAYFARING STRANGER

African-American Spiritual

181. ESSENTIAL ELEMENTS QUIZ – SCALE COUNTING CONQUEST

PERFORMANCE SPOTLIGHT

182. AMERICA THE BEAUTIFUL – Band Arrangement

Samuel A. Ward
Arr. by John Higgins

183. LA CUCARACHA – Band Arrangement

Latin American Folk Song
Arr. by John Higgins

PERFORMANCE SPOTLIGHT

184. THEME FROM 1812 OVERTURE – Band Arrangement

Peter Illyich Tchaikovsky
Arr. by John Higgins

PERFORMANCE SPOTLIGHT

Solo with Piano Accompaniment

Performing for an audience is an exciting part of being involved in music. This solo is based on *Serenade in G Major, K. 525*, also known as "Eine Kleine Nachtmusik" ("A Little Night Music"). **Wolfgang Amadeus Mozart** wrote this piece in 1787, the same year the American Constitution was signed into law. You and a piano accompanist can perform this for the band or at other school and community events.

185. EINE KLEINE NACHTMUSIK – Solo *(Concert E♭ version)*

Wolfgang Amadeus Mozart
Arr. by John Higgins

DUETS

Here is an opportunity to get together with a friend and enjoy playing music. The other player does not have to play the same instrument as you. Try to exactly match each other's rhythm, pitch and tone quality. Eventually, it may begin to sound like the two parts are being played by one person! Later, try switching parts.

186. SWING LOW, SWEET CHARIOT – Duet

African-American Spiritual

187. LA BAMBA – Duet

Mexican Folk Song

RUBANK® SCALE AND ARPEGGIO STUDIES

ALTO SAXOPHONE KEY OF G (CONCERT B♭) *In this key signature, play all F#'s.*

1.

2.

3.

4.

ALTO SAXOPHONE KEY OF C (CONCERT E♭)

1.

2.

3.

4.

RUBANK® SCALE AND ARPEGGIO STUDIES

ALTO SAXOPHONE KEY OF D (CONCERT F) *In this key signature, play all F#'s and C#'s.*

RHYTHM STUDIES

RHYTHM STUDIES

44

CREATING MUSIC

THEORY

Composition

Composition is the art of writing original music. A composer often begins by creating a melody made up of individual **phrases**, like short musical "sentences." Some melodies have phrases that seem to answer or respond to "question" phrases, as in Beethoven's *Ode To Joy*. Play this melody and listen to how phrases 2 and 4 give slightly different answers to the same question (phrases 1 and 3).

1. ODE TO JOY

Ludwig van Beethoven

2. Q. AND A. *Write your own "answer" phrases in this melody.*

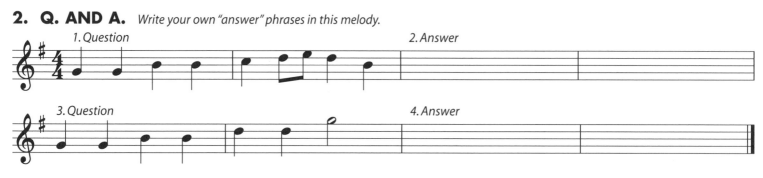

3. PHRASE BUILDERS *Write 4 different phrases using the rhythms below each staff.*

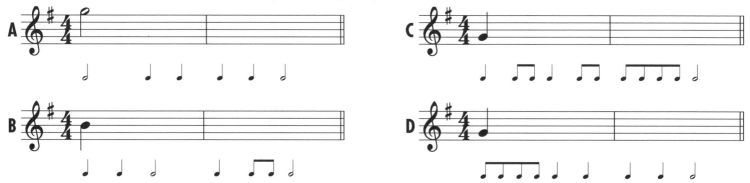

4. YOU NAME IT: _____

Pick phrase A, B, C, or D from above, and write it as the "Question" for phrases 1 and 3 below. Then write 2 different "Answers" for phrases 2 and 4.

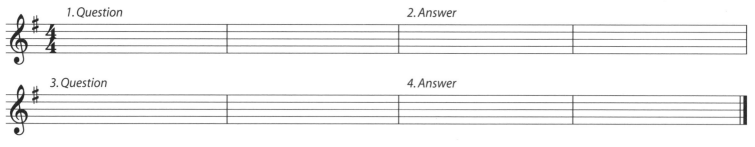

THEORY

Improvisation

Improvisation is the art of freely creating your own melody *as you play*. Use these notes to play your own melody (Line A), to go with the accompaniment (Line B).

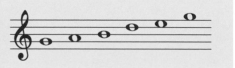

5. INSTANT MELODY

 You can mark your progress through the book on this page. Fill in the stars as instructed by your band director.

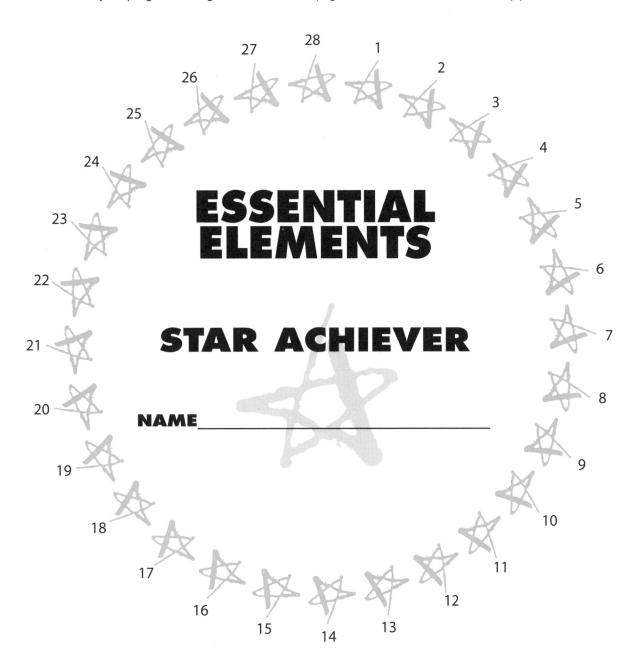

ESSENTIAL ELEMENTS

STAR ACHIEVER

NAME_____

MUSIC — AN ESSENTIAL ELEMENT OF LIFE

FINGERING CHART

E♭ ALTO SAXOPHONE

Instrument Care Reminders

Before putting your instrument back in its case after playing, do the following:

- Remove the reed, wipe off excess moisture and return it to the reed case.
- Remove the mouthpiece and wipe the inside with a clean cloth. Once a week, wash the mouthpiece with warm tap water. Dry thoroughly.
- Loosen the neck screw and remove the neck. Shake out excess moisture and dry the neck with a neck cleaner.
- Drop the weight of a chamois or cotton swab into the bell. Pull the swab through the body several times. Return the instrument to its case.
- Your case is designed to hold only specific objects. If you try to force anything else into the case, it may damage your instrument.

○ = Open
● = Pressed down

The most common fingering appears first when two fingerings are shown.

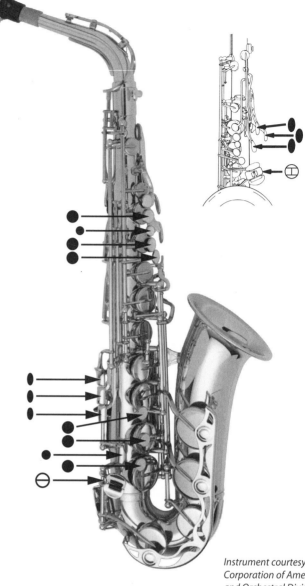

Instrument courtesy of Yamaha Corporation of America, Band and Orchestral Division

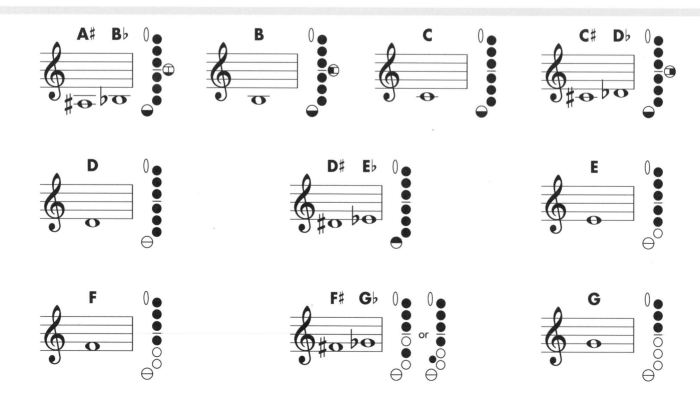

FINGERING CHART

E♭ ALTO SAXOPHONE

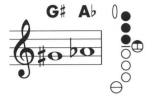
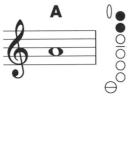
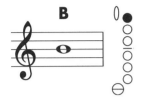
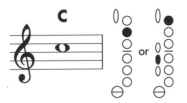
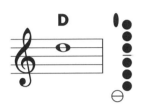
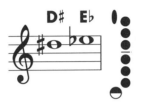

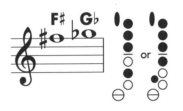
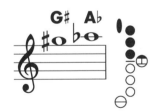
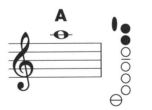
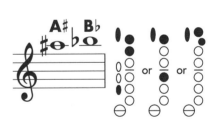
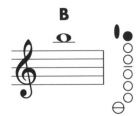
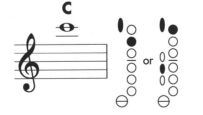
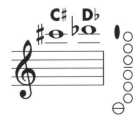
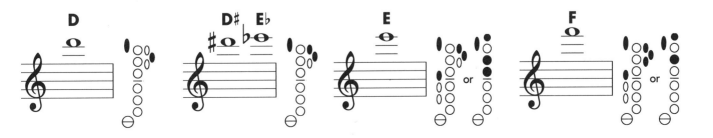

REFERENCE INDEX

Definitions (pg.)

Composers

World Music